A Tale of One Well in Malawi

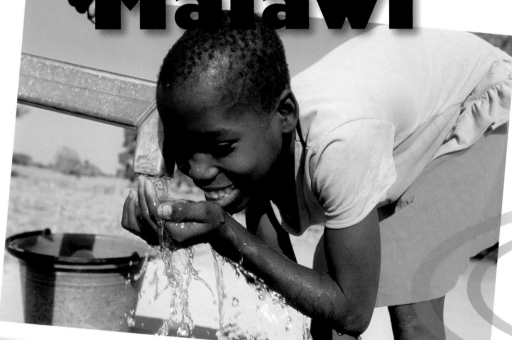

CAPSTONE PRESS
a capstone imprint

the
BIG
PICTURE

Sarah Levete

First Facts is published by Capstone Press, a Capstone imprint,
151 Good Counsel Drive, P.O. Box 669, Mankato, Minnesota 56002.
www.capstonepub.com

First published in 2010 by A&C Black Publishers Limited, 36 Soho Square, London W1D 3QY
www.acblack.com
Copyright © A&C Black Ltd. 2010

Produced for A&C Black by Calcium. www.calciumcreative.co.uk

032010
005746ACF10

Library of Congress Cataloging-in-Publication Data
Levete, Sarah.
  A Tale of One Well in Malawi / by Sarah Levete.
    p. cm. — (Big picture)
  Includes index.
  ISBN 978-1-4296-5506-4 (library binding)
  ISBN 978-1-4296-5516-3 (paperback)
 1. Groundwater—Juvenile literature. 2. Water—Juvenile literature.
 3. Animal-water relationships—Juvenile literature. 4. Animal-water
relationships—Malawi—Juvenile literature. I. Title. II. Series.

  GB1003.8.L48 2011
  363.6'1—dc22   2010008902

Every effort has been made to trace copyright holders and to obtain their permission for use of copyright material.

This book is produced using paper that is made from wood grown in managed, sustainable forests. It is natural,
renewable and recyclable. The logging and manufacturing processes conform to the environmental regulations
of the country of origin.

Acknowledgements

The publishers would like to thank the following for their kind permission to reproduce their photographs:

Cover: Shutterstock: Louie Schoeman (front); WaterAid (back). **Pages:** Dreamstime: Atm2003 3, David Snyder 18;
Istockphoto: Michelle Gibson 20–21, Ai-Lan Lee 6–7; Pump Aid: 16–17, 18–19, 23, 24; Shutterstock: Lucian Coman
2–3, Alistair Cotton 19, Pichugin Dmitry 4–5, Leksele 12–13, Geir Olav Lyngfjell 15, Silver-John 22–23, Urosr 6,
Viki2win 13, A. Vogler 14–15; WaterAid: 1, 5, 9, 8–9, 10, 11, 17, 20.

Contents

Who Needs Water?

Can you get a glass of water whenever you need it? In some parts of the world, people can't.

Meet Asale

*"My name is Asale. I live in Malawi in **Africa**. Malawi is a hot country with little rain. It is hard to find water here."*

Hi!

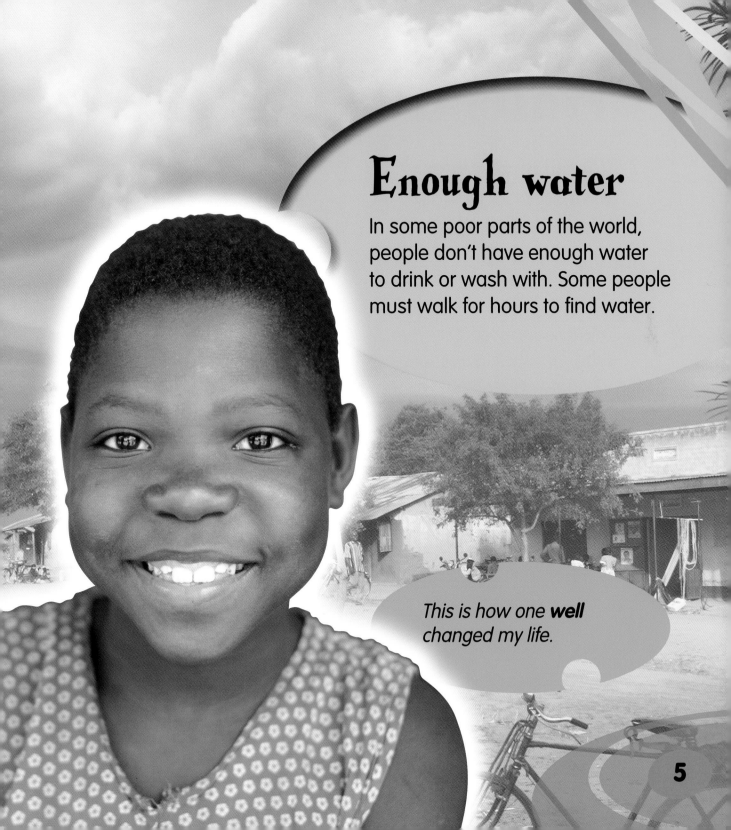

Enough water

In some poor parts of the world, people don't have enough water to drink or wash with. Some people must walk for hours to find water.

*This is how one **well** changed my life.*

Water for Life

People need water to drink and to wash. Water is also needed to grow food.

Asale says

*"People in my country need water for their **crops** to grow. We grow most of our own food."*

People need water to grow bananas.

Can't make it

You can't make water! All of our water comes from rainwater that falls into rivers and lakes. Rainwater also collects deep underground.

It's raining!

A Long Walk

Many people in other parts of the world don't have faucets at home. They have to walk to rivers or lakes to get water.

Asale says

"Before the well was built, my friends and I walked for three hours to reach the nearest river."

Not much fun...

Missing out

Children like Asale miss out on school when they spend the day fetching water.

Fetching water is hard work.

Dirty Water

Many people in poor parts of the world have to get dirty water from rivers or lakes.

Asale says

"Before the well was built, all our water came from the river. The water was dirty and muddy."

Muddy water

Getting sick

Imagine drinking water from a river that animals bathe in and leave **waste** in. It's full of **germs** that make people sick.

Many children only have dirty river water to drink.

11

No Rain

When there are long hot times without rain, the ground and rivers dry up. This is a drought.

Asale says

"My country is getting hotter. It means there is even less water to go around."

Hot, hot, hot

Can't store it

In rich parts of the world, water is stored in **tanks**. Malawi cannot afford to build tanks to store water during a drought.

The ground is dry and cracked during a drought.

Thirsty Animals

When there is a drought, it is hard for people to find enough water for their animals to drink.

Asale says

"We take our animals to the river so they can drink water. But if the rain does not fall, there is no water in the river."

No rain, no water

No food

Thirsty animals can die. People in Malawi need their animals for meat and milk. If the animals die, people can die too.

People and animals need water to drink.

15

The Well

A well is a deep hole dug into the ground. The inside is covered with special material. This keeps the water in the well clean.

Asale says

*"Grown-ups in the village raised some money for a well. A **charity** helped us build the well."*

When the well is finished, Asale and her family will be able to drink clean water.

Clean water

Deep water

There is lots of water deep under the ground. The well is built near some of this water. The water flows into the well.

A Better Life

Wells change people's lives. If people don't have to walk to fetch water every day, they have much more time.

Asale says

"The well has changed everything for me. Now I have more time to go to school and to play."

More time

The well helps the villagers to have more time to work and to earn money. Life is better for everyone.

People in Asale's village now have more time to grow food.

19

Every Drop...

We can't make new water,
so we must use it carefully to
make sure everyone has enough.

Asale says

*"If people in rich countries keep using
too much water, there will not be enough
for people in poor countries like mine."*

*Children everywhere
need clean water to be
happy and healthy.*

Save it

You can help to save water.
Try having a shower instead
of a bath, or turn off the faucet
when you brush your teeth.

Water for everyone

Glossary

Africa a huge area of land called a continent. Africa has many countries.

charity an organization to help people

crops plants that farmers grow for food

drought a long time without rainfall

germs things that make people ill

tanks large containers that hold water

waste pee and poop

well a deep hole dug into the ground. Water from underground flows into the well. The well fills up with water.

Further Reading

FactHound offers a safe, fun way to find Internet sites related to this book. All of the sites on FactHound have been researched by our staff.

Here's all you do:

Visit www.facthound.com

FactHound will fetch the best sites for you!

Books

Water for Everyone by Sally Morgan, Franklin Watts (2007).

Water Water (Window on the World) by Paul Harrison, Zero to Ten (2010).

Index